OTL 928M

Vintage Cars
IN COLOR
Phil Drackett

Cathay Books

CONTENTS

Two of the greatest names of the vintage period are Alfa-Romeo and Mercedes. On this page is a 1931 Alfa-Romeo roadster. The previous page shows a 1927 K-type Mercedes tourer and the endpapers illustrate a 1936 drophead Mercedes-Benz Sedanca 500K.

INTRODUCTION

The Roaring Twenties were the days of jazz trumpeters, trousers known as Oxford bags, American bootleggers dealing in illicit liquor and a dance called the Charleston. They were also the days of fast, elegant and luxurious cars as well as lightweight, economy cars. The memory of those cars – and sometimes the cars themselves – are treasured today by thousands of motoring enthusiasts, lovers of machinery in the grand manner. Thus, appropriately enough, many of them are known as vintage cars and are appreciated in much the same manner as vintage wine.

Collecting, cultivating, preserving and admiring old cars is now a worldwide hobby, but to the newcomer the various categories of car can be confusing, especially since the terms and periods involved tend to vary from country to country. In the United States, for example, the two main clubs for enthusiasts have the words 'antique car' and 'horseless carriage' in their titles, terms which are not used officially in the British Isles. However, most countries adhere to the definitions laid down in Britain.

A *veteran car* is one manufactured prior to 31 December 1916. Of these, the *true veterans* are those built before 31 December 1904, and the remainder are known as *Edwardian veterans*. Only the first group are permitted to take part in the world-famous London to Brighton Run for veteran cars which takes place each November.

Vintage cars are those manufactured after 1 January 1919 but before 31 December 1930. The reason for the three-year gap is that few cars other than military vehicles were manufactured during the period when World War I reached its peak.

Apart from vintage cars proper, certain selected cars of a later date are known as *post-vintage thoroughbreds*. These are models which the appropriate clubs have decided have more merit than the typical mass-production models of the 1930s. Some of the cars of this period which qualify for the PVT designation are Alvis, Aston Martin, Frazer Nash and Rolls-Royce.

The vintage car was born out of the adversities, trials and tribulations of World War I, nurtured by the native genius of American, British and Continental designers, and succoured or inhibited by the taxation policies of various governments, according to the individual viewpoint.

The wartime use of aluminium in aircraft engines, particularly for pistons, was followed up by many automobile manufacturers. Some of these engines were failures, others outstanding successes. The six-cylinder AC engine, to quote one instance, employed an aluminium block. It went into production in 1921 and was still going strong in the 1950s.

World War I also provided a proving ground for many touring cars, ranging from the Baby Peugeot, designed by Ettore Bugatti, to the 4½-litre 25/30 Crossley, thousands of which were used as staff cars, tenders and ambulances. The armoured cars used by the British army in the desert were based on Rolls-Royce chassis; this experience provided valuable information for post-war car designers.

Heavy motoring taxation was introduced in many countries and in Great Britain, for example, this led to the development of smaller and more efficient engines. The desire for speed also brought

The 1934 Hispano-Suiza (below) *was probably the only car which in its day was mentioned in the same breath as Rolls-Royce.*

about the general adoption of brakes on all four wheels, something which had existed only on a few French racing cars before the war.

However, the major development during the vintage period was the general introduction of electrical equipment. Cadillac had marketed an electric starter as early as 1912 – indeed their British representative, Fred Bennett, had won several awards for demonstrating the wonders of these American cars – but it was not until after 1918 that electric starters and lighting equipment began to appear on cars manufactured in Europe.

To many the term vintage car automatically relates to sports cars and there is no doubt that the vintage period produced a great many outstanding examples in this category. Frazer Nash and Aston Martin were great names in Britain; Bugatti and Alfa-Romeo on the Continent. But there were many others: the wonderful Hispano-Suiza, of which the Tulipwood model was probably the most beautiful car ever built; the Vauxhall Velox, usually referred to these days as the 30/98 because Vauxhall later gave the Velox name to a pedestrian saloon; the legendary Bentleys; and the 12/50 Alvis which remained in production for some eight years. There was also the Lancia Lambda which became very popular as a fast touring car during this period.

Taxation and economic conditions caused a remarkable collection of economy cars to be manufactured, some of them justifiably called cyclecars. In the economy class the British G.N. and the French Amilcar were amongst the most successful but the cheap American car gained in popularity throughout the world. The Model T Ford was the obvious leader but the Overland, Dodge, Studebaker and Chevrolet all did well.

The Americans provided very tough competition for the British market; the Model T Ford cost only £120 in Britain at a time when the native Austin Seven Chummy cost £150. The Peugeot, Citroën, Renault and Fiat, although selling well in their home countries, were handicapped by import duties when it came to foreign sales.

Despite the limitations imposed by governments, the vintage period nevertheless produced many of the world's great cars and no enthusiast can fail to be stirred by their names; many of them still live on in our motoring industry today.

The 1925 6-cylinder Locomobile (below) *was a vintage product under a name known earlier for outstanding steam cars. The Mercedes poster* (right) *had some justification for the claim 'The car with the extra class'.*

7

ARISTOCRATS

There are some cars which stand out above all others, cars which are truly aristocrats of the automobile world. Many flourished during the age of the vintage car, though some did not survive that period. Two of the greatest cars were the Rolls-Royce Phantom II (left) and the Duesenberg J; both are 1931 models. Other names, such as Bugatti, Hispano-Suiza, Peerless and Pierce-Arrow, are no longer around, though many of the cars illustrated here are still in evidence, provided money is not a barrier to ownership.

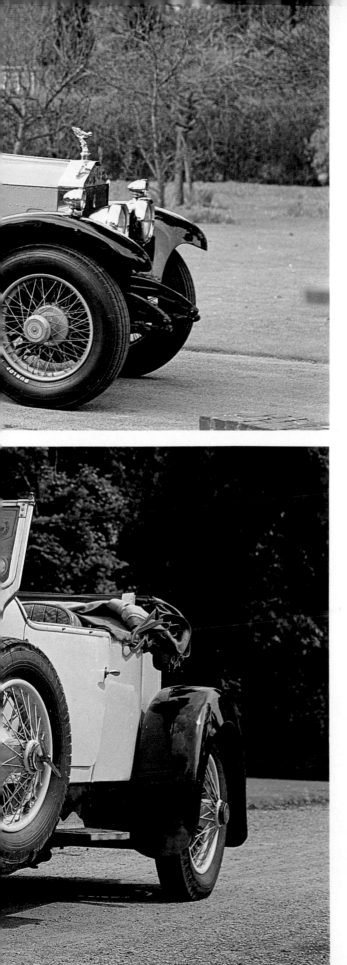

Few would argue that the Silver Ghost is not the most famous model in the Rolls-Royce range. The last of the Silver Ghosts (*left*) was produced in 1925. They were first produced in 1906 and boasted a high level of refinement, including such a low noise-level that the claim was made that the only sound you could hear in a Rolls was the ticking of the clock. Despite being far ahead of its contemporaries, the Silver Ghost was not as costly as some other cars. It had a 7-litre, 6-cylinder engine of 'square' design.

Rolls-Royce came into being through the partnership of Rolls, a daredevil motor-racing and flying pioneer, and Royce, a brilliant engineer. Rolls was killed in a flying accident soon after the partnership began but Royce went on to build the 'world's best car'. The famous 'Spirit of Ecstasy' radiator mascot was suggested by another motoring pioneer, the second Lord Montagu, and designed by Charles Sykes, the model being Lord Montagu's secretary. About 2,500 Ghosts were built before it was succeeded by the Phantom I in 1925, which gave way to the Phantom II in 1929. There was also the smaller Rolls Twenty which appeared in 1922 and became the 20/25 in 1925 (see page 22).

A car of comparable quality was the Swiss-designed Hispano-Suiza, which was built in France and Spain. Alas, the car has not continued in production but the memory lingers on. *Below left* is the 1919 Hispano-Suiza, a car which marked a great step forward in the luxury class. When it was shown at the Paris Salon in 1919 it took the lead over its rivals because of its all-round powerful servo brakes; it was the first luxury car to be so equipped. A great asset for Hispano-Suiza in their post-war manufacturing of motor cars was the knowledge accumulated during the war through the manufacture of high-powered aircraft engines.

One of the marque's most famous models was the 'Boulogne', so-called because on 2 September 1923, Hispanos of this type finished first and second in the Circuit de Boulogne race for the Boillot Cup. In the same year the winning car, driven this time by André Dubonnet instead of the Boulogne winner, Garnier, was victorious at San Sebastian. Dubonnet then bought a 'Boulogne' from the factory, lowered the chassis and the radiator, and had a special ultra-streamlined body built. The resulting Tulipwood Hispano was probably the most beautiful car ever made. Its owner entered it for the tough Sicilian road race, the Targa Florio, but it was unsuited to the many hairpin bends and finished only fifth.

Another great European car of the vintage period was the Mercedes which, happily, like the Rolls, is still in production today. *Below* is the typical top-of-the-range touring car of the period, the 1927 Mercedes-Benz. An interesting feature on this model is the dual windscreen.

Mercedes started life as Daimler but the name was changed in a bid to defeat sales resistance from the French. It was thought that the Germanic-sounding Daimler only fanned the hatred France had for the Germans.

Across the Atlantic there were few cars which could rank with the great Europeans but, nevertheless, such US companies as Packard, Peerless and Pierce-Arrow (The Three Ps), Cadillac, Marmon and Mercer did manufacture some fine automobiles. The 1929 Pierce-Arrow cabriolet (*right*)

is shown with typically American white-walled tyres. The term 'cabriolet' refers to a car with a leather hood and glass windows which wind down into the panelling. The interior of the car tended to be draughty and the hood awkward to get down, so the cabriolet eventually disappeared from the scene.

Pierce-Arrow was at its peak just before World War I and did well in reliability trials, but it lost money in the late twenties and came under the control of Studebaker.

A popular type of body was the sedan, as on the 1929 Marmon straight-eight (*overleaf*). The Wall Street crash was disastrous for Marmon, and they went out of business in 1933. Their problem was that the cars were too expensive for the masses and not luxurious enough for the rich.

The Wall Street crash and the subsequent world-wide financial depression ruined many car manufacturers, yet, perhaps surprisingly, the best but also one of the most expensive of them all, Rolls-Royce, carried on. The 1930 Rolls-Royce Phantom is pictured *below* with the mascot clearly shown. In 1931, Rolls-Royce took over another prestige British manufacturer, Bentley, whose fame had largely been won on the race circuits of Europe with several victories in the Le Mans 24-hour race, and an immortal drive for third place against genuine Grand Prix cars by Tim Birkin in the French Grand Prix. Sir Henry (Tim) Birkin was Britain's outstanding driver of the period.

Vauxhall was another old-established British manufacturer with a reputation for good cars. The genius behind the outstanding Vauxhalls was Laurence Pomeroy Snr, who took a fine example of the Vauxhall, the 4-litre D-type 'Prince Henry', bored the engine out to 4½ litres, redesigned the brakes and the electrical system, and produced the classic Vauxhall, the 30/98 (*right*). Launched in 1919, right at the beginning of the vintage era, the car was an immediate success. As a tourer the car was capable of 136 km/h (85 mph), while in racing trim, the 30/98 was capable of 160 km/h (100 mph). Between 1920 and 1923, the 30/98 won 75 races, was runner-up 52 times and third 36 times.

Pictured *below* is the beautifully styled 1931 Cord L-29 cabriolet. During the vintage years, the United States did produce some remarkable men in the motor-manufacturing industry. One name, little known today, was that of E. L. Cord, who joined the Auburn automobile company in 1924, as General Manager. He soon revived the flagging fortunes of the company. He had a gift for picking talented designers and engineers, amongst them Gordon Buehrig, still spoken of with awe in the American industry. This allowed Cord to produce some wonderful cars, including the first American front-wheel-drive car to gain popular approval, a car in which designer Harry Miller played a leading role.

The L-29 was introduced by Cord in 1929 to bridge the gap between his comparatively low-price Auburns and his millionaire-bracket Duesenbergs. It was a front-wheel drive car with a straight-eight Lycoming engine – Lycoming being another company Cord had absorbed. The car was a disaster from the beginning, primarily because not enough planning and preparatory work was done before it was put on sale. In time the troubles might have been sorted out but the Depression hung over the industry and in the three years it was in production, few of these models were built. The L-29 had one outstanding merit – beautiful styling.

In the twenties, Cord was offering cars with a guaranteed speed of 160 km/h (100 mph). Cord moved to England during the Depression but soon returned to America where, in 1937, his company finally failed. He left the memory of three great cars: the Auburn, the Cord and the Duesenberg, which Cord had taken over during 1926–7.

The Chrysler, named after another quite remarkable motor manufacturer, has survived to the present. On the *right* is the 1931 version, and if it looks un-American, it is because it is fitted with British Carlton coachwork.

Milan by Maserati and sold in the U.S. by Chrysler.

Chrysler insiders who have seen prototypes enthusiastically describe the planned $25,000 super coupe as "a cross between a Ferrari 308 and a Porsche 928" and say the car may debut by spring 1987.

If that weren't enough to whet the appetites of aficionados, Maserati still has a few tricks of its own to unveil.

Import veteran Kjell Qvale (rhymes with "Kamali"), Maserati's San Francisco-based U.S. importer and chairman of DeTomaso Industries, says the company plans to launch at least three new versions of the Maserati Biturbo in the first half of 1985. These include a high-output Biturbo S, a luxury Biturbo 425 sedan and a two-passenger Biturbo convertible, with body by the Italian coach-building firm Zagato. Prices will range from $26,000 for the basic twin-turbo coupe to about $35,000 for the roadster.

Qvale

The $65,000 Quattroporte luxury sedan, created by Italian designer Giugiaro and introduced in 1979, won't be replaced in the U.S., Qvale says, until the 1987 model year, when Maserati will offer a four-door, twin-turbocharged, 3.5-liter version of the Biturbo's V6

An exotic arrival

Best news for fans of the Maserati marque is the arrival — not before '88, hints Qvale — of an exotic $75,000 coupe to do battle against longtime adversaries Ferrari and Lamborghini.

"We don't want to abandon Maserati's traditional image of luxury and tremendous performance," says the Norwegian-born Qvale, one of whose non-automotive companies manufactures circuit boards for the Trident missile.

The new coupe, he adds, will feature state-of-the-art technology and "will be more advanced than anything on the road." Qvale won't say if Maserati will select another wind name for its new creation.

Perhaps they'd consider "Mistral's daughter" . . .

PIONEERS

Hundreds of different types of car were manufactured during the twenties and thirties. Some were cars which, for one reason or another, were pioneers – cars which introduced a feature which was to influence car design and performance in the future. One such car was the 1922 Bullnose Morris (below), first conceived in 1913, and so named because of the shape of the radiator.

The Austin Seven (*above*), better known as the 'Chummy' or 'Baby Austin', became one of the most successful and long-running cars in the history of the automobile. The open version is shown here. It had four-wheel brakes and a claimed fuel consumption of 21 km/l (60 mpg). 'Baby' was an obvious description, and 'Chummy' came from the close proximity in which the two rear-seat passengers had to sit. The car was surprisingly well made despite its cheapness. It also achieved many successes on the race track and in the sphere of record-breaking. An upright saloon was introduced in 1926, and by 1929 the tourer cost only £125. It was made on licence in Germany as BMW, in France as Rosengart and in the United States as Bantam.

Austin owed its name to Herbert (later Lord) Austin, a country boy who, after working for the Wolseley sheep-shearing company in Australia, returned to England and designed cars for Wolseley when they turned to motor manufacture. He left them in 1905 to set up on his own and by the outbreak of World War I, the Austin Motor Company was Britain's number one firm. In the aftermath of war, Austin, like other companies, had to struggle to survive. Austin's genius saved the company, however, when he devised this tiny, inexpensive car.

On the *left* is the 1925 Rolls-Royce Twenty coupé. It was a small Rolls which first appeared in 1922.

Perhaps the most successful pioneer car was Ford's Model T (*left*). Millions were built and for many years more Model Ts were being registered in the USA than all other makes of car combined. And yet the car was sold to the public with only the barest essentials and few, if any, of the accessories and trimmings a modern-day motorist would expect with a car. Therefore a whole sub-industry grew up around the Model T, with small fortunes being made.

One pioneering feature of the Model T was that it was the first American car, apart from a few 'one-off' makes, to have the steering wheel on the left-hand side. In the summer of 1908, the car cost $850, then the equivalent of £170, and was considerably cheaper than previous Ford models. The Roadster version, which followed in 1909, had a bucket seat for one in the rear and this had no protection against the weather so, not surprisingly, humorists soon labelled it the 'mother-in-law' seat. Convertible and coupé versions followed but basically the Model T remained the same. One last effort was made by Henry Ford in 1927 to bolster sales and maintain the popularity of the car. The result was the car pictured here, the 1927 Model T coupé. The gasoline tanks were finally removed from under the front seat, balloon tyres were fitted, wire wheels were made available and, at long last, a real choice of colours was offered.

The Opel rocket car (*below*) was never in mass-production. Opel were leading German manufacturers of both Grand Prix and road cars for a long period and are still in business today as the German branch of General Motors. However, this 1928 Rak 2 rocket car was 40 or 50 years ahead of its time, not only in conception but also in body-work. It could easily be taken for a racing car of the immediate post-World War II period. But in 1928 the whole idea of rocket propulsion was greeted cynically and abortive record attempts only served to confirm the public's attitude. Today, of course, all the world's land-speed records are held by jet-propelled machines, the modern equivalent of Opel's rocket.

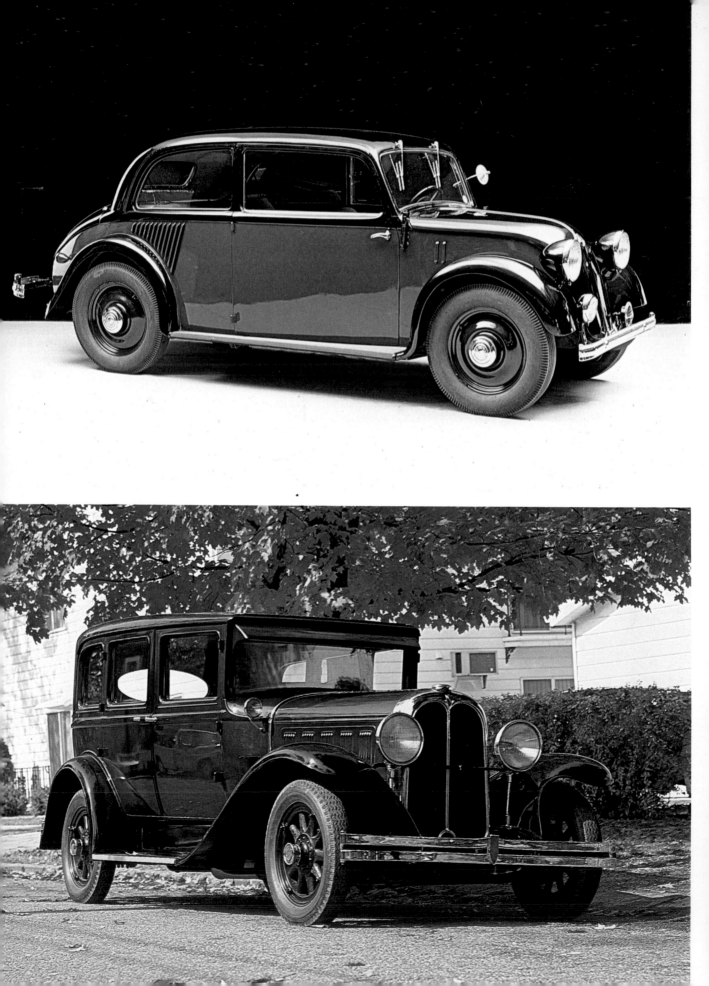

Some vintage fashions continued into the post-vintage period. *Above* is a rumble seat on a 1936 Auburn coupé. The first car with a rear engine was the 1933 Mercedes 130H (*top left*), and the 1929 Essex 4 saloon (*below left*) was an American attempt to break into the family market.

The vintage years were times of experiment in the motoring industry, and inevitably failures resulted as well as successes. The USA alone produced more than 3,000 different makes of car. One car which remained prominent throughout the period was the French Amilcar, one of the best light cars based on the rather dubious cyclecars which flooded the market just after World War I. Sold at a reasonable price, the Amilcar with its flared wings and pointed tail, a pioneer of streamlining, enjoyed considerable popularity for a number of years.

Armstrong-Siddeley cars enjoyed a reputation for hard wear and reliability but, during the vintage years, they lacked the glamour which many of their rivals possessed. Nevertheless the firm was awarded Britain's top automotive trophy, the Dewar Trophy by the Royal Automobile Club, after an 18 hp tourer averaged 725 km (450 miles) per day for 23 days. The average speed was 39 km/h (24 mph), the fuel consumption 8 km/l (24 mpg), oil 4,725 km/l (13,347 mpg) and the car used only 6.8 l (1½ gal)

of water. It retained the original tyres throughout.

The French Ballot company concentrated on production models and produced a 2-litre, 4-cylinder-engined car which enjoyed considerable success. Another French company, Voisin, was noted for elegant and expensive vehicles although they tended towards the big and heavy. For a number of years after the war they produced only the 22/30 Knight-engined model, but it was beautifully made and very fast for the time. In 1921 it was capable of 113 km/h (70 mph) and indeed averaged 80 km/h (50 mph) between Paris and Nice. The boat-decked tourer set a fashion emulated by many other manufacturers.

In complete contrast to the Voisin were the cars of the British Rover Company. Although, after World War II, their cars were referred to as 'the poor man's Rolls-Royce', their vintage cars were more down-market. In the early years their business was built on the 2-cylinder Rover Eight which, although described by the critics as crude and cheap, was sparing on petrol and sold well.

The Lincoln was among the finest cars money could buy in the twenties, and when Henry Ford took over the company in 1928, he maintained its reputation for top quality. The 1937 Lincoln Zephyr (*overleaf*) had a powerful V-12 engine.

27

THE MEN BEHIND THE CARS

The years of the vintage car were the years in which many great designers and manufacturers came to prominence. In some cases the firms they founded and the cars that evolved are still with us today; the ideas which these men of vision brought forth were the foundation of the prolific motor age which was to follow.

GIOVANNI AGNELLI

The Agnellis, for instance, are a family which controls a motor manufacturing empire vitally important to the prosperity of Italy. Giovanni Agnelli was a 33-year-old cavalry officer with a penchant for engineering when he joined a group of prominent citizens of Turin to found *Fabbrica Italiana Automobile Torino* which soon became F.I.A.T., and then Fiat.

In the pioneer days, Agnelli's giant racers won fame for Italy and orders for the factory. A variety of cars followed, ranging from the luxurious and the sporting to the tiny economy cars. And as Fiat grew into one of Italy's major industrial organizations, the company swallowed up Lancia and Ferrari, both companies which had been set up by well-known racing drivers. Fiat were among the pioneers of industrial welfare and are still noted today for the care they take of their employees. The firm has always been headed by an Agnelli, with Edoardo following his father, and grandson Giovanni now in control.

WALTER OWEN BENTLEY

Walter Owen Bentley, generally known as WO, was a railway apprentice who, after achieving success as a motorcycle trials rider, went into business as concessionaire for three French car manufacturers and began racing and record-breaking. During World War I Bentley served in the Royal Naval Air Service and, when he was given scope to develop his talents, he designed the Bentley rotary aero-engine.

After the war WO formed the Bentley Car Company which, with a string of victories in the classic 24-hour race at Le Mans, upheld the prestige of British motor racing in the twenties and thirties. The Bentley Car Company was eventually taken over by Rolls-Royce but the new company, Bentley Motors (1931) Ltd, continued to make quality cars for a number of years.

ETTORE BUGATTI

Another brilliant designer to achieve fame on the race circuits of the world was Ettore Bugatti. Although his cars carried the blue racing colours of France, Bugatti was born in Milan in 1881 and he remained an Italian citizen until shortly before his death.

In Milan he won eight out of the ten races he entered on a twin-engined tricycle he built himself. On the strength of this he was offered a job by De Dietrich, the motor manufacturing company, and moved to Alsace which was then in German territory. He was to spend most of his life there. From the moment a Bugatti finished second in the 1911 French Grand Prix, the blue-painted cars went from success to success. In 1925–6, for example, Bugattis won 1,045 events; in 1927, 806 races and hill-climbs. Five times in succession Bugattis took the Targa Florio in Sicily.

Bugatti also built luxury cars; the Royale was a classic, and he designed the Baby Peugeot years before its counterpart, the Baby Austin, appeared in Britain. Bugatti had other interests including horse-riding, boating and sculpture – the famous Bugatti radiator is based on a horseshoe.

WALTER PERCY CHRYSLER

Chrysler represented the American dream: he was a farm boy from Kansas who became one of the world's outstanding industrialists. He began his working life as a railway cleaner in the workshops of the Union Pacific railroad in Ellis, Kansas, and by his mid-thirties he was plant manager of the American locomotive works, which had a car manufacturing subsidiary. He was recruited by the ailing General Motors Corporation in 1912, and four years later he was general manager of the Buick division. By the end of World War I, he was one of America's top 12 industrialists. Later, he revived the Maxwell firm and used it as a basis to build a car which bears his name; the first Chrysler appeared in 1924.

ANDRÉ CITROËN
A brilliant engineer and businessman, a genius at public relations, André Citroën founded the company which bears his name and which today is in alliance with Peugeot and Talbot.

Citroën first became involved in the motor industry in 1907 when he rescued the French racing-car firm of Mors from financial disaster. During World War I he became a French national hero when he organized the manufacture of shells for the French war effort, and when the war ended he switched to the manufacture of motor cars.

Among the many remarkable achievements claimed for him are: the first modern assembly-line in Europe (1919); the first European car with an all-steel body (1924); and the first European manufacturer to use flexibly mounted engines, as devised by Chrysler in the USA (1931).

HENRY FORD
An even more important dynasty was founded by an American, Henry Ford. Son of an Irish immigrant farmer, young Henry took a dislike to farming after a fall from a horse. He built his first crude quadricycle in 1896, and followed this with a racer and won the so-called World Championship at Grosse Pointe. He then designed and built two monster machines, on one of which the legendary Barney Oldfield won the Manufacturers' Challenge Cup in 1903. As a result of this success, Ford Motors was founded. In rapid succession Ford produced Models A, B, C, F and N; nearly 10,000 of the N model were sold. Ford dreamed of a light, four-cylinder touring car of not less than 20 hp which could carry up to five people. Thus, in 1908, the

Model T was launched, probably the most famous car in the history of motoring. Made without any trimmings, it sold by the million, and continued to sell, year after year. Ford introduced the conveyor-belt assembly-line in 1913 and did not halt the production line even for a coat of paint. 'You can have any colour you like as long as it's black,' he was reported to have said.

Ford will be remembered as the man who established the eight-hour working day, guaranteed a minimum wage and brought motoring to the masses. Still one of the world's leading manufacturers, Ford Motors have never relinquished their connections with motor sport and their Ford-Cosworth engine has won more Grands Prix than any other engine in history.

WILLIAM MORRIS
Typical of the early designers and manufacturers is William Morris, later Lord Nuffield, who played a similar role in Great Britain to that of Henry Ford in the United States. Forced by his father's illness to give up ideas of becoming a surgeon, William left school at 15 and with a capital of £1 set up as a bicycle repairer in the back room of his family's home in Oxford High Street.

He moved on to repairing cars and motorcycles, opened a garage, and built the Bullnose Morris. Cars like the MG Midget and Magnette, the Morris Eight, the Cowley, the Oxford and others followed. In 1934 he became the first motor manufacturer to be raised to the peerage. Later, his company merged with Austin to become the British Motor Corporation, forerunner to today's British Leyland. William Morris, like Henry Ford, gave a great deal of money to charity.

Men like these, and Austin, Renault, Olds, Cord, Lanchester, Durant and Marmon built most of the great cars of the vintage period, but also, alas, some of the bad ones.

SPORTING CARS

The twenties and thirties were great years, not only for
out-and-out racing cars, but for roadsters with racing
performance and fast-accelerating sports cars which could
hold their own in the toughest hill-climb competitions.
They were also great years for record-breakers. And in
the forefront of these activities was the Mercedes. The
1928 SSK Mercedes illustrated here is typical of the style
and class. It won numerous races, including the 1930
Irish Grand Prix and 1931 German Grand Prix.

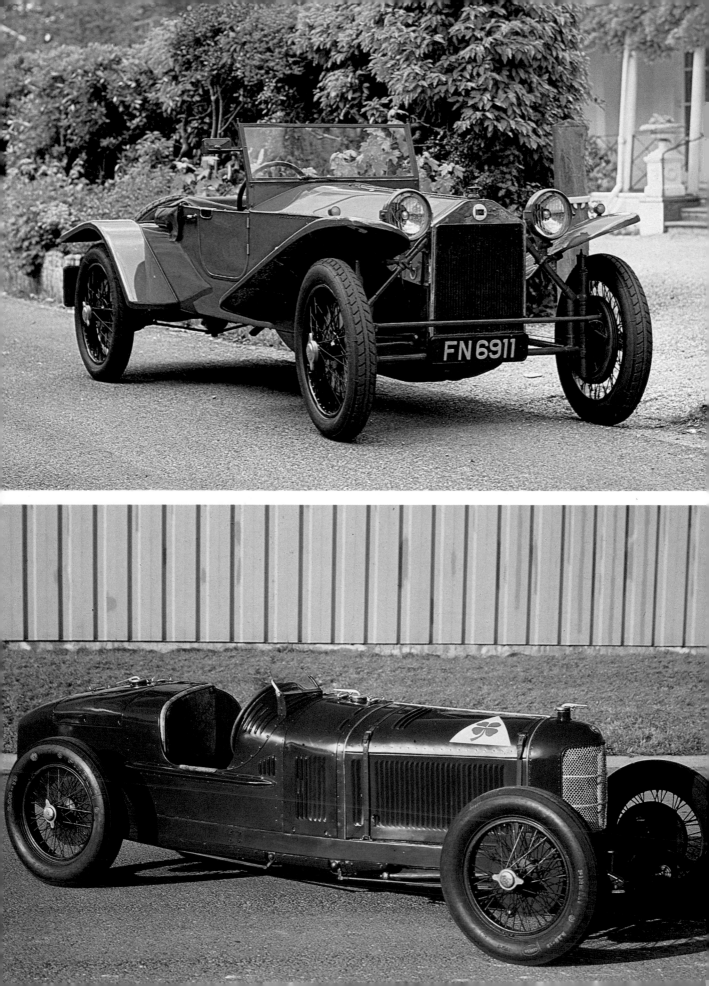

The Lancia firm was founded by the famous Italian racing driver and although the Lambda (*top left*) was first shown at the Paris Salon in 1922 (the model shown here is 1924), and marketed as a touring car, it was a fast one, exceeding 113 km/h (70 mph) at a time when its contemporaries were doing 88 km/h (55 mph). Its roadholding was good and it boasted a new system of independent front suspension which was the first marketed on a large scale. However, it proved disappointing in long-distance trials which were then very popular, being hampered by its low build and great length.

A real Italian racer, the Alfa-Romeo P2 Grand Prix car (*below left*), was introduced in 1924 with a straight-eight engine. It won the 1924 French Grand Prix and was undefeated for the rest of the season. In 1927, Formula racing was suspended and the P2 was modified for greater power and won 7 races out of 30 in 3 years, second only to Bugatti which won 15.

Ettore Bugatti probably produced the greatest racing cars of all time. One of his early triumphs was the Type 13, introduced in 1912. In 1921, four cars of this type finished in the first four places in the Brescia race and subsequently Bugatti marketed the car as a Brescia Bugatti. A 1926 version is pictured here (*above*).

Two other Bugattis of the vintage era, which were on sale to the ordinary motoring public, were the Type 43 Grand Sport of 1927 which was the production edition of the 35B Grand Prix car, and the 1930 Type 50 supercharged 8-cylinder, capable of more than 185 km/h (115 mph). This car reversed the process and the following year was converted into a Grand Prix car. Bugatti's racing triumphs were numerous, but towards the end of the vintage period he produced what he regarded as his masterpiece. His firm was prospering, his racing cars had just won the classic Targa Florio for the fifth successive year and so he unveiled the most elegant, luxurious, high-grade car ever to be produced. This was La Royale – often referred to as 'Golden Bug' since the prototype was much gilded. The prototype was first seen in 1926 with a Packard body fitted to the Bugatti chassis. The 8-cylinder engine weighed 355 kg (7 cwt) and, with a wheel-base more than 4.5 m (15 ft) long, the car could comfortably accommodate a 7-passenger body. Weighing more than three tonnes in all, La Royale was still capable of 193 km/h (120 mph). Three years later Bugatti decided to launch it on the world but the economic crisis struck and only six or seven were built. At least four of these cars are in the USA in museums and private collections.

The 4½-litre Bentley made its Le Mans debut in 1927 and was expected to win, but a multiple crash eliminated not only the 4½-litre but some of its rivals too. The car won the race in 1928, with Tim Birkin at the wheel (*above*). These big sports tourer-bodied Bentleys may have looked cumbersome beside the racing Bugattis, but they outclassed French opposition time after time. The last one was produced in 1931, the year the company was taken over by Rolls-Royce.

The 1931 Brough (*above right*) was a British sports car with pleasing lines and good performance. In body design it was ahead of its rivals and it was also equipped with a good performance Meadows engine. However, it never became a success.

The French Delage firm produced excellent fast tourers in the 2- to 3-litre range, although their speciality in the twenties was racing cars. A typical Delage roadster (*below right*) looks both smart and powerful. Delage designed a Grand Prix car for the 2-litre formula in 1922 and in 1925 had the satisfaction of being acclaimed world champions after winning three out of six Grands Prix. For the 1½-litre formula, they also produced a straight-eight, which proved to be one of the world's outstanding racing cars. It lost to Bugatti in 1926 but, modified, proved nearly invincible the following year, Delage winning four out of five major races. Ten years later, British racing driver Richard Seaman had a most successful season with one of these cars.

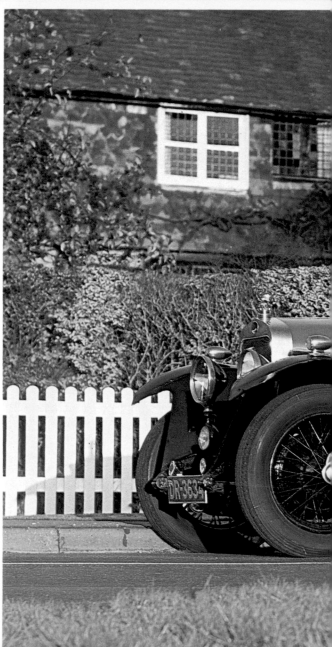

The 1931 Fiat Spyder (*above*) is typical of the European sports cars of the period with its hood and wire wheels. The Fiats as road models were always regarded as good and durable, and the lighter cars were very lively for their weight. In winning the 1923 Italian Grand Prix, Fiat made history by being the first super-charged car to win a major Grand Prix. However, after 1927 they withdrew from racing to concentrate on road models.

In Britain, with the possible exception of the Riley, the MG (*top right*) was undoubtedly the most popular of the smaller sporting cars. 'Old No. 1' was a sports two-seater, vintage 1925, and unmistakably betrayed its origins with the bullnose radiator, but this was later replaced with a much smarter, flatter radiator which was divided into two segments. The very first MG (the letters stand for Morris Garages) was built in 1923 with a Hotchkiss engine fitted to a Morris chassis. It was capable of more than 129 km/h (80 mph). Many models followed, all with 14 hp, until 1928 when a cheaper and smaller model was introduced. This was the MG Midget. Typical of this breed was the MG TA in the picture.

In contrast to the MG, the Invicta (*below right*) was a large (3-litre and $4\frac{1}{2}$-litre), fast and expensive sports car with rapid acceleration. The model pictured here is the 1931 tourer version. It did not make an entrance until 1925 when it was capable of 129 km/h (80 mph). Later it was developed into a genuine 160 km/h (100 mph) car. In racing, its record was not impressive – it was doing well in the 1929 Le Mans when a con rod broke – but it did perform well in reliability tests and trials. Violet Cordery was awarded the 1927 RAC Dewar Trophy after driving a 3-litre Invicta on a 10,000 mile world tour. Two years later she and her sister created a record by being awarded the Trophy again, this time for driving a $4\frac{1}{2}$-litre car 50,000 km (30,000 miles) in 30,000 minutes, a remarkable achievement.

The vintage era ended in great triumph for Invicta. Donald Healey won his class in the 1930 Alpine Trials and then he won the Monte Carlo Rally outright in the following year. Later he was to make his mark as a manufacturer of Healey sports and racing cars. He did much for the prestige of British sports cars at that time.

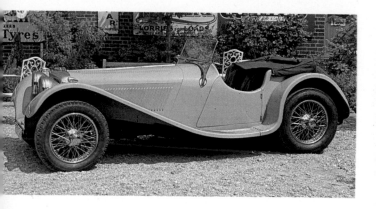

A British company which just squeezes into the vintage period but whose great days lay ahead was the SS, later to be called Jaguar. William Lyons founded the Swallow Sidecar Company in 1922, when he was 21. In 1927 he began manufacturing car coachwork in addition to sidecars, and in 1931 produced his first car, the SS (*above*). Four years later came the Jaguar, and in 1945 the company took its name from this car. Apart from the long-bonneted SS One, there was a smaller coupé, the SS Two. Lyons also made the Wolseley Hornet Swallow and the Austin Seven Swallow Mk II. The SS One and the SS Two were discontinued in 1936, being replaced by the new SS Jaguar models.

The company which produced the 1937 Riley Sprite (*right*) commenced the vintage years with a small 4-cylinder, 10.8 hp car. Five years later came the 'Redwing', 1½ litres and much more sporting, and then in 1926 came the 1100 cc Riley which was to form the basic model for a long time. It has been described as a pioneer version of the modern high-efficiency light car and, with its low build, rugged chassis and sound brakes, it sold well. At £235 for the touring version in 1927, it cost more than the Swift (£210) or the Clyno (£160), but was a car of considerably greater merit. Six thousand were on the road by 1929, most of them being fabric saloons which were known as the 'Monaco'. Record-breaking designer Reid Railton evolved a shortened and lowered version known as the Brooklands, which could do about 145 km/h (90 mph). It was an indication of the possibilities of the Riley, which were fulfilled in the thirties when Rileys achieved many racing successes, notably in the Tourist Trophy races. Later, the excellent ERA, a racing single-seater, was developed from the basic Riley theme.

By 1938 financial failure had overtaken the firm and it merged with Morris, MG and Wolseley to form the Nuffield Group. The Riley name continued to be used, however, until 1970.

The outstanding sports car of the thirties was almost certainly the German BMW 328, a 1938 version of which is shown racing in the photograph *above*. The BMW was to continue its success after World War II and became one of the most respected road cars. The top echelons of racing in the thirties were dominated by the Germans. With vast sums of state aid from the Nazis, the white and silver Mercedes and the Auto-Unions won nearly all the major races.

The car which made the breakthrough for Mercedes, after a season in which Auto-Union had shone, was the 1937 Mercedes 125 (*top left*). It was also the year in which the former mechanic, Hermann Lang, won the first two races of the season, at Tripoli and the Avus, for Mercedes. Lang survived the war and was still driving Mercedes in demonstration runs in the seventies.

The post-vintage Aston Martin models were all made at Feltham, Middlesex, near London. The racing car (*below left*) is the 1936 version of the marque. Aston Martin was a name derived from the original designer Lionel Martin and the Aston Clinton hill-climb. Despite the magic of this name, the company had a rather chequered career in the early days, as indeed it has in modern times. The company resumed production after World War I in 1920 when they produced a 1½-litre side-valve car which was fairly expensive. Although cars were only produced in small numbers, the marque became quite well known through the racing exploits of Count Zborowski and Clive Gallop, especially in 1922 when a second place in the Brooklands 200 Mile Race and several world and class records were achieved. The company changed hands in 1926.

43

ECONOMY CARS

Some vintage cars might be sneered at by enthusiasts, and yet they still have their place in motoring history because they filled, or attempted to fill, a need: a need for a comfortable family car; or for an economical car; or an economy car with a sporty look. One such need was filled by this Buick saloon, a family car yet impressive enough when chauffeur-driven.

The 1924 5 cv Type 172 (*below*) was Peugeot's answer to the 5 cv Citroën. The baby Peugeot had been designed for Peugeot by Bugatti before World War I but did not make an appearance until the war ended. Instead, Peugeot introduced the Quadrilette which, if it could not be called a cyclecar, seemed just as ridiculous an object since it seated only two people, one behind the other. The Quadrilette was so narrow as to be unstable, so in 1922 the seats were staggered. The engine was a tiny 680 cc but nevertheless the car remained popular in France, albeit slightly heavier and larger, until about 1930.

In 1922 André Citroën brought out the 5 cv two-seater, a perky little car which was followed in 1923 by the three-seater, the famous 'Cloverleaf' model (*below right*). This 7.5 hp car certainly had a quaint appearance and no performance to speak of but it was economical to run and extremely reliable. With the earlier Baby Peugeot and the small Fiats, it was one of the few foreign cars to establish a hold in Britain. In the USA, there was little demand for such a small car.

The Fiat 501 was produced as early as 1919; the 1922 version is pictured here (*top right*). It was generally considered to be one of the most pleasing small family cars ever made. The steering and brakes were good and the side-valve engine was remarkably quiet and refined. The 509, which was a sensation at the Paris Show in 1925, was another beautifully made light car. Unlike the Citroën, the 501 carried four people, two of them in the rear 'dickey-seat', great for romance providing it was not raining.

The overwhelming demand in the twenties was for lower-cost economy cars and this was initially met with a rash of cyclecars – 'children's pedal cars fitted with lawnmower engines' was how one critic described them. Some, like the Amilcar, survived but the majority were swamped by the genuine small cars pictured on these pages. In Great Britain the Austin Seven (page 23) was a classic example of the new breed. Other light cars proliferated on the British market, among them names such as Calcott, Clyno, Stellite and the better known Humber, Swift, Standard and Wolseley.

Some people wanted economy cars but not economy appearance. In some cases manufacturers put more pleasing coachwork on their economy cars for a modest increase in price, and in other instances, specialist manufacturers provided new bodies. A vintage example of this was the 1927 Austin Swallow (*below left*), which was shaped more like a drunken bee. It was produced by William Lyons' Swallow Sidecar firm and was regarded as quite glamorous at the time.

Worthy and solid are the adjectives that come to mind in surveying the 1928 Bean (*top left*). Popular demand was not confined to very small cars, however. Many motorists had large families, so the Morris, the very popular Austin 12/4 and the Hillman and Standard Fourteens had a good share of the market in Britain. At least three post-war firms tried to get into this market in Britain but the Angus-Sanderson and the Cubitt soon disappeared

from the fray. The Bean, however, was well thought of by a number of motorists and survived until 1929, when the Depression finished it as it did so many other cars. The other problem was matching the competitive price of Morris cars.

Renault retained their distinctive bonnet through most of the vintage period, as can be seen from the elegant and surprisingly large-looking 1927 6 cv (*below*) which had an engine of less than 1000 cc. Renault also firmly believed in promoting reliability as the main selling point for their products and in the thirties they were advertising their cars in the following manner: 'Look underneath the cars you buy . . . No car may be judged from superficial appearance alone. Graceful lines and a pretty body are valueless unless based on a chassis designed from every point of view to stand up to hard service.' The headline on the advertisement read 'Enduring Quality'.

The Singer (*above*) and the Standard Big Nine (*below right*) made their debut in 1928, along with the Morris Minor, Triumph Seven and the Clyno. (The cars pictured here are both 1931 models.) These five vehicles sold for less than £200 each. The Singer had to survive the witticisms about sewing machines, but it did have an overhead camshaft engine, as did the Morris Minor. This would have been unheard of on a car of this category a few years earlier. The brakes on all five were superior to those on earlier light cars and the Triumph was one of the first British cars to use an hydraulic system. All five had surprisingly lively performance but this was achieved at the expense of low gear ratios and high-speed engines. Cheapest of the quintet was the Clyno Nine – in 1929 the price was down to £112 10s, a remarkable sum

for a fully equipped four-seater saloon. The Clynos were simply made and easy to drive. The withdrawal of the Rootes group as their selling agent lowered the boom on the Clyno Engineering Company in 1929. The Standard Nine was followed in 1936 by the Flying Nine, a streamlined fastback version.

The Depression had an even greater effect on American manufacturers and Packard, who until then had made nothing but top-quality cars, had to compromise to survive. An example from this period is the 1930 Sedan (*top right*). At their peak in 1928, Packard sold 50,000 cars, and were the most widely distributed luxury make. In order to keep their top range of cars in production, they introduced these cheaper models – the prestige of the quality cars sold the cheaper ones.

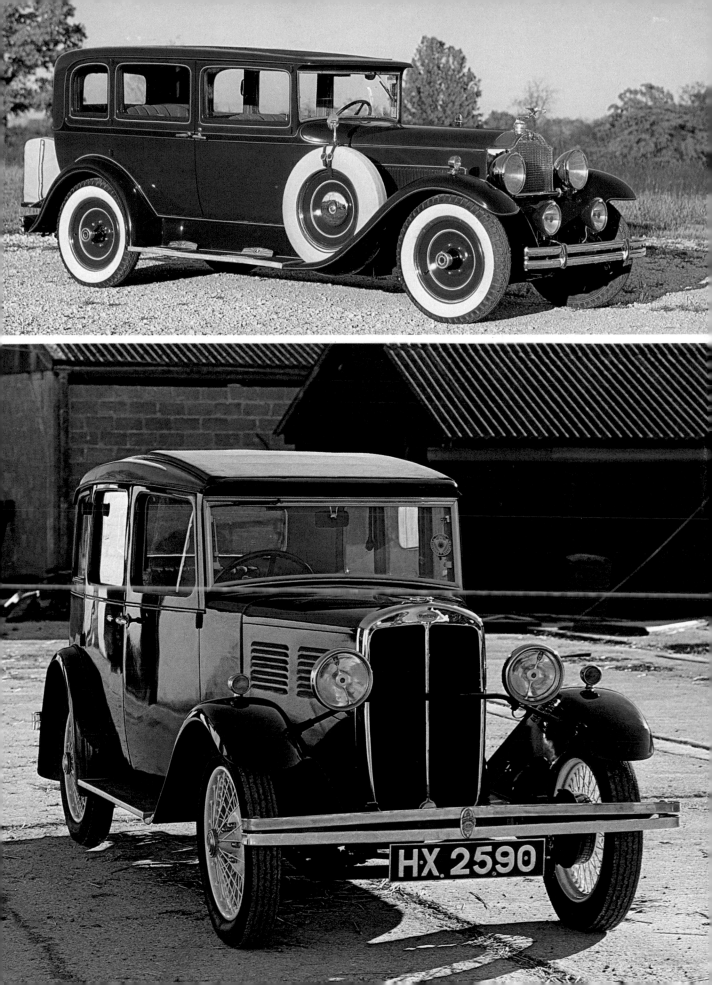

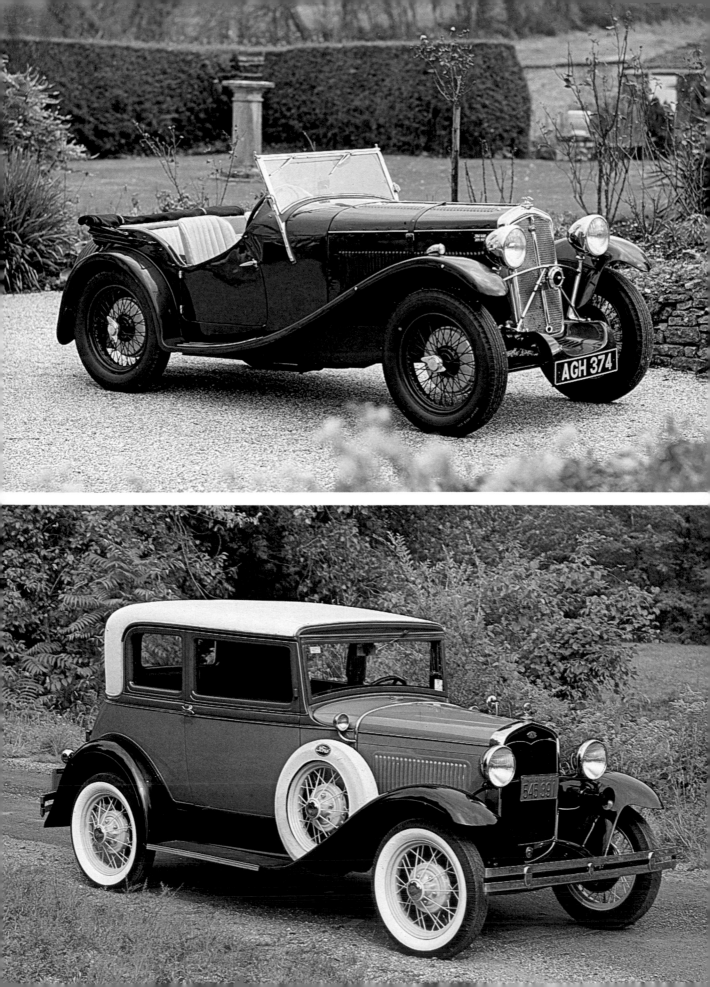

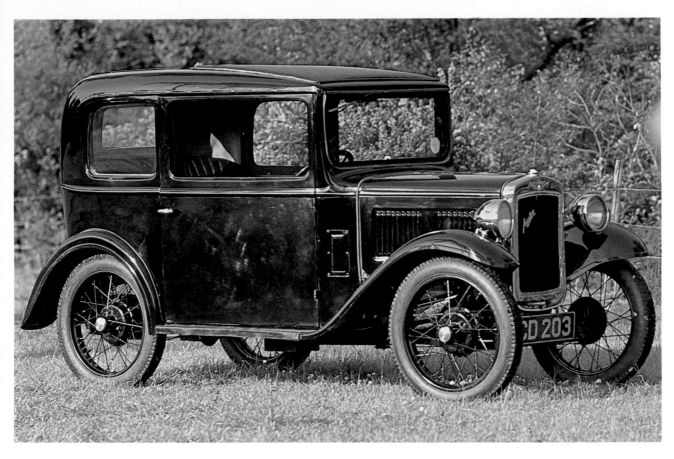

While other companies failed, the Ford empire motored happily on. The Model T finally expired despite Henry's valiant efforts to revitalize it, but the success of the Model A (*bottom left*) justified the claims his son Edsel had made for it. The A had great popularity for three years or more after its introduction, and finally convinced Henry that the public wanted four-wheel brakes and three-speed transmissions. The A also had wire wheels. In most respects it was an excellent car, but it suffered at the hands of motoring historians because it did not equal the record of its illustrious predecessor, the Model T.

The small, relatively cheap, 6-cylinder 1933 Wolseley Hornet Special (*top left*) was a speciality of the company in the early thirties. It was the smallest 6-cylinder car on the market. The Austin Seven Saloon of 1933 (*above*) was another effort to fit the family into an economical automobile, and it was still in production in 1939.

In most motor-manufacturing countries, the Depression meant the end of the vintage period and quite clearly marked a decisive phase in the history of the automobile. The field was being left to major manufacturers, most of whom survive to the present day: in Britain, Austin and Morris; in France, Citroën, Peugeot and Renault; and in Italy, Fiat.

Mass-production was firmly entrenched, hence the reason that from 1931 onwards enthusiasts would tend to sneer at cars made after that date and give their acclaim only to a handful of post-vintage thoroughbreds. Before leaving the vintage light cars, however, there are some deserving mention. Humber, a former bicycle company, continued car manufacture into modern times but during the vintage period they were notable for high-quality cars in the light-car field. In 1922 came the Humber 8/18 with a 985 cc engine which was smooth and efficient. It had only a 3-4 seater, in other words a 'chummy' body, and in 1925 the firm brought out the 9/20 with a slightly larger engine and much bigger body. Front-wheel brakes were added in 1927 and in 1929 there was further enlargement, but saloon coachwork turned it into a rather ordinary car. Few of the 30,000 cars made before 1930 still exist.

Jowett of Bradford made their first car in 1910. The flat twin water-cooled engine was slightly enlarged after the war and then was made in virtually the same form until 1953, one of the longest production runs on record. Apart from saloon cars, the firm also used their engines in Bradford vans. In 1937, Jowett introduced their first 4-cylinder engine.

One of the great cars of all time was the Citroën traction avant 7 cv (*below*, the 1938 model) and the 1937 roadster version (*right*). The 7 cv model had independent suspension, front-wheel drive and unitary construction. The words 'traction avant' heralded a significant development in the history of the motor car. It was not strictly a vintage development in execution although it was in development. In the USA, Christie pioneered front-wheel drive on cars as far back as 1904 and in Europe, J. A. Gregoire worked on the principle between the wars. Neither of them had been able to persuade manufacturers to adopt the idea on a large scale. It was up to André Citroën to introduce this revolutionary design to his cars in an effort to boost post-Depression sales. As his own design department had come up with nothing new, Citroën had turned to a young engineer André Lefebvre, then working for Renault. He had designed Voisin's 1923 Grand Prix car and had then driven it to finish in the French Grand Prix. Lefebvre brought the idea of a front-wheel drive car with him to Citroën in 1933. Citroën took a gamble and dismantled his factory in preparation for the production of the new car. To celebrate, he held a party for 6,500 guests, although he could ill-afford it as his company was badly in debt. The success of the new car could save him.

By April 1934 the Citroën traction avant was in full production. It was a low-slung car, the first front-wheel drive car in quantity production. It had a monocoque body, replaceable wet-cylinder liners for the suspension block, torsion-bar and independent front suspension. It sold well, but the complaints rolled in. So hurried had been the development programme that the car was unreliable. The company was swamped by warranty claims and officially declared bankrupt. The car of course became one of the greats but André Citroën died before this success was realized.

POST-VINTAGE

The end of the vintage era did not necessarily mean that no more great cars were built. Shining like jewels amongst the lesser lights were such cars as this magnificent 1933 Duesenberg SJ roadster, with a body by Walton. The Duesenberg's race-bred heritage shows through every sleek line of one of the world's most elegant automobiles.

Typical of American cars of the period is the 1933 La Salle (*below*). Interesting features include the external sun-visor, spare wheels on both running boards, and twin external rear-view mirrors. This type of car was very popular as a town car, often being chauffeur-driven.

Of greater acclaim and more sporty appearance was the 1936 Auburn 852 straight-eight (*overleaf*). Both the 851, which preceded it, and the 852 were labelled 'speedster' by their designer Gordon Buehrig. Each car bore a plaque on the dashboard certifying that it had been tested at over 160 km/h (100 mph) before delivery. Unfortunately the speedsters were sold at a loss and the rest of the Auburn range did not sell in sufficient quantity to keep the plant going. The Auburn disappeared forever in 1936, shortly after its stable-mates the Duesenberg and the Cord.

The Rolls-Royce was still in demand, including this 1933 20/25 saloon (*top right*), though the rather outlandish Wylder coachwork does not make it the most elegant Rolls.

The Austro-Daimler shown (*bottom right*) is the 1932 version and truly a classic car. Like the Rolls, the Austro-Daimler was pronounced a superb car in the vintage period and towards the end of this era a sporting version, driven by Hans Stuck, was sweeping all before it in international hill-climbs.

The lines for the PVT designation (post-vintage thoroughbred) were rather strictly drawn but not all the cars produced after 1931 can be dismissed out of hand, although most cars of the thirties were strictly utilitarian – a means of transport, mass-produced and tailored to meet the pocket of the majority of ordinary drivers. These considerations have remained the major concern ever since.

The Daimler (*below left*) had challenged Rolls-Royce as manufacturers of the best of all English cars since before 1914, but had never succeeded in wresting the laurels from them. A chain-driven Daimler had won the classic Shelsley Walsh hill-climb in 1905 but after that all trace of the sporting image disappeared and the car became associated in most people's minds with limousines for the royal family and hearses for the dead. Touring and coupé coachwork was sometimes fitted, as in the car shown here, but always seemed a little out of place on such a marque. Nevertheless, Daimler produced many models: in 1927 they offered 23, mostly variations on the theme, since often a Daimler of one year was almost indistinguishable from another 10 or 15 years younger. Innovations came towards the end of the vintage era when the Vauxhall genius, Laurence Pomeroy Snr, took over at Daimler and reorganized their design department. Gradually the Knight engine was replaced by more conventional but modern power units, and the famous fluid flywheel was introduced in conjunction with a preselector gearbox, giving greater smoothness and ease of control. However, the Daimler has never truly captured the hearts of vintage-car enthusiasts.

On the Continent the formidable trio of Mercedes (*overleaf*), Bugatti (*above*) and Alfa-Romeo (*above left*) was still leading the classic field in the thirties. The Italians, especially, saw that many great cars, though more or less mechanically the same, could be given an enormous advantage over others in the world marketplace if they had exotic styling and coachwork design; and so began the era of the great creative artists. Probably the first and best was Pinin Farina, whose work has turned many ordinary automobiles into fantasies. Typical of his earlier work is the Alfa-Romeo which is illustrated here.

The 1934 Bugatti Type 37 (*above*) also illustrates this principle. Unlike the Alfa, the running board has been retained but the wings have been given a smoother, more flowing treatment. An unusual aspect of the design is the extreme backward slope of the windscreen, in contrast to the very upright rear window. The other outstanding design feature is the use of two contrasting colours in the paint-work, which rivets attention to the car.

The 1931 swing-axle 170 Mercedes (*overleaf*) also uses contrasting colours as a design feature, although other new design treatments had not yet reached Mercedes by this time.

INDEX

Figures in italics refer to illustrations.

Acknowledgements

Unless mentioned below, all photographs are
by Nicky Wright.
Andrew Morland: half title; Peter Roberts:
7, 16, 17, 20–21, 23 right–25 below, 34
below, 36 above, 38, 40 left, 42–43, 46, 49, 59
below, 62 above; Rainer Schlegelmilch: 26
above, 32–33, 64; J. Spencer Smith: 48
below, 54–55 below.

**First published in 1980 by
Cathay Books
59 Grosvenor Street, London W1**

© 1980 Cathay Books

ISBN 0 86178 058 2

Produced by
Mandarin Publishers Limited
22a Westlands Road,
Quarry Bay, Hong Kong

Printed in Hong Kong

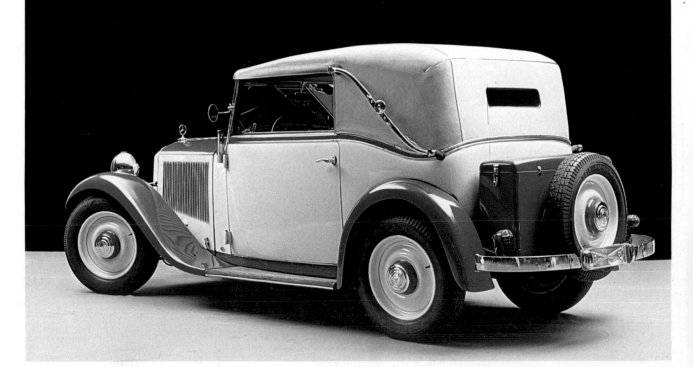